A Celtic Daily
Prayer Companion

DAVID ADAM

Marshall Pickering
An Imprint of HarperCollins*Publishers*

Marshall Pickering is an Imprint of
HarperCollins*Religious*
Part of HarperCollins*Publishers*
77–85 Fulham Palace Road
London W6 8JB

First published in Great Britain
in 1997 by Marshall Pickering

1 3 5 7 9 10 8 6 4 2

Copyright in this compilation © 1997 David Adam

David Adam asserts the moral right to be
identified as the compiler of this work

A catalogue record for this book is
available from the British Library

0 551 030623

Printed and bound in Great Britain by
Woolnough Bookbinding Limited,
Irthlingborough, Northamptonshire

CONDITIONS OF SALE

Contents

Introduction

Over the last twelve years, I have been thrilled by the number of people who have told me of how their vision of the world has been enlarged and their lives extended. Many people have talked about renewal in their prayers and a coming home in their faith. Some have come quite excitedly saying, 'I feel I am praying for the first time with my whole being' or 'Somehow I have known this way of prayer all my life, yet I am now using it properly for the first time.' Nearly all these people have been talking about their discovery of Celtic prayer. Most have rejoiced in its homeliness and simplicity, in its earthiness and love of the world. One person said to me, 'This is prayer of the home and is at home in the home.' Indeed, for many it was like coming across a long lost treasure which they felt was theirs by inheritance and right. Just as the Celtic Christians brought light to the Dark Ages, we see them bringing light to many of us again.

The Celtic church was never separate from the rest – I hardly even like talking about 'Celtic spirituality' – but the Celtic peoples brought a

special richness to the Church in their expressions of prayer and art. As the world has been enriched by the Celtic artwork that surrounds their copies of the Scriptures, especially the gospels, so it is enriched by their earthiness in their prayers. The prayers of the Celts were far more like the prayers of the Hebrews than of the classical cultures of the Romans and Greeks. Both Celts and Hebrews were rich in imagery and symbol, both refused to divide heaven from earth, both were aware of an underlying unity in all things, and both were sure of a God who was in their midst and concerned about their everyday affairs. Many of the prayers are of the home rather than a church, or of daily work in the open air and fields rather than a fixed building. The words are the ordinary language of conversation rather than a special exalted way of talking. Though people are struck by the earthiness of these prayers, there is also a feeling of majesty and awe. This is not a trivialized God, a God who is lowered to our level, but a God of great mystery who makes demands, a God who transforms all that He touches. It is not a bringing down of God but an uplifting of the people who come to Him. This is a God whom it is exciting to discover, to know and to love: a God who is life-enhancing and life-extending, a God who enriches the whole of our being.

The prayers I have chosen in this book have all been used in my prayer life and in my teaching. Each has enriched my life at some time or another. They have seen me through the good times and the bad, through times of hope and times of darkness. These prayers have been chosen because they look at each phase of life in the presence and power of God. They are a great reminder that, although we cannot see Him, our God never leaves us or forsakes us. If only we will come to Him we can begin to discover the joy of being children of God. Because our modern world

so often ignores Him, it expresses loneliness and hopelessness as a major part of its daily existence. So many people seem lost and do not know where to turn. We need to know again the source of our life and the very foundation of our being. We need to find a path to our Creator, Redeemer and Sustainer: we need to rediscover the way that leads to peace. Again, for many, the Celtic way of praying has proved to be a path of light, a way back to God.

These prayers are not meant to be read so much as learnt by heart. I am a great believer in 'Recital Theology' – we need to get the truths we say we believe in into our hearts and minds. They are prayers to be said aloud and out of our innermost being. Nearly all these prayers were handed down in communities and families, passed from heart to heart. Hear these words from Catherine Maclennan, a crofter of Moydart:

> My mother taught us what we should ask for in prayer, as she heard it from her own mother, and as she heard it again from the one who was before her. My mother would be asking us to sing our morning song to God down in the back-house, as Mary's lark was singing it up in the clouds, and as Christ's mavis was singing it in the yonder tree, giving glory to the God of the creatures for the repose of the night, for the light of the day, and for the joy of life. She would tell us that every creature on the earth below and in the ocean beneath and in the air above was giving glory to the great God of the creatures and the worlds, of the virtues and the blessings, and would *we* be dumb! (*Carmina Gadelica* III, p. 25)

So often feelings and emotions can tell us lies, we can feel forsaken and alone when that is never true, we can feel that God is far off when He is always close at hand. So we need to teach heart and mind to train them in the right way. Recital theology is a good way of doing this, affirming the truths of our life and of the presence and power of God, and at the same time acknowledging that God will make demands of us. This is not positive thinking but a tuning of our minds to the reality of our God. Affirming the presence and protection of God at each part of the day extends our vision and helps us to see more clearly our place in the world. Such praying gives a rhythm to our lives. Listen to these words from the Hebrides:

> When the people of the Isles come out in the morning to their tillage, to their fishing, to their farming, or to any of their various occupations anywhere, they say a short prayer called 'Ceum na Còrach', 'The Path of Right', 'The Just or True Way'. If the people feel secure from being overseen or overheard they croon, sing, or intone their morning prayer in a pleasing musical manner. If, however, any person, and especially if a stranger, is seen in the way, the people hum the prayer in an inaudible undertone peculiar to themselves, like the soft murmur of the ever-murmuring sea, or like the far-distant eerie sighing of the wind among the trees, or like the muffled cadence of far-away waters, rising and falling upon the fitful autumn wind.   (*Carmina Gadelica* III, pp. 48–9)

Here is the suggestion that people and nature are at one in prayer. When they pray they express a unity of all creation that is so often hidden from

us. Our world is a fragmented world and in it people are so easily broken. We need to discover the underlying unity and the wholeness that is our birthright as children of God – this is not something we create; the underlying unity is there for us to discover and to rejoice in.

One of the great things about prayer is its striving for reality; prayer is not an escape from what is going on but rather an immersion of ourselves deeper into all that is happening. When things are going wrong it is no use pretending that all is going well – we have to acknowledge the fact that we are in the dark. It is for this reason I was attracted to the prayer by Alistair Maclean in his book *Hebridean Altars*, which begins '**Though the sun rise cheerless on this isle today**'. Long before I came to live on a small island I knew the meaning of these words. The world around us can so often be a cheerless isle with great clouds forming all around us, and we ourselves can be a cheerless isle with darkness billowing up from inside us. We have to admit that this is reality – well, part of it. We can enter into darkness and storm so easily and, suddenly, without warning, we then find that we cannot cope and we are plunged into weakness, sickness or distress. For no reason of our own a great dark cloud comes upon us. Because I am a countryman and love the open spaces, at times like this I think of the words of Yeats:

Come away, O human child!
To the waters and the wild
With a faery hand in hand,
For the world's more full of weeping than you can understand.

I was not looking for the faery! But I did seek out that 'other world' which the Celtic Christians found ever so near. I learnt that to get away from all the noise and clamour of the world was to be given a breathing space, a time to think and a time to feel. So often the world will regiment us and tell us how we ought to act and react. It is necessary to escape from this so that we can be ourselves, we need space and freedom to be the people we are truly called to be. It is too easy to be so immersed in the things of the world about us, that we lose sight of the greater world that is ours. Making space, and praying, opens us up to the greater dimensions that are about us. Perhaps it is because they thought of themselves as on the very edge of this world that the Celts decided the other world must be close at hand. Time and time again Celtic peoples were pushed out of their homeland and into the wilderness. Often they were oppressed and forced into remote regions that were thought to be on the very edge of the world. But they learnt that when they were on the very edge of life or of the world, another world was there and breaking in. In Celtic folk tales, especially the Irish ones, it seems it is so easy to fall into that other world. An unseen world is ever near, just beyond the horizon. Built into the Celtic way of thinking was the expectation of another world that was interwoven with theirs, and either that could break into their world or they could enter it. The incarnation expresses this fact of a God who is ever present and yet comes in a special way. The God who is beyond our sight – and yet in our midst. A God who is there, though a cloud may hide Him from our sight. Just as the sun is in the sky on the darkest day, we need to learn that God never leaves us or forsakes us. No matter what happens to us, our God is with us. For the Celtic Christians, even when they are driven to the edge of life or hope they affirm the love and

protection of God. So Alistair Maclean's prayer affirms, '**Though the sun rise cheerless on this isle today, my spirit walks upon a path of light**'. That is reality: though storms rage and troubles beset us, though we feel overwhelmed and are overwhelmed, our God is still with us – so we walk in a path of light. We affirm with St Paul, 'Nothing can separate us from the love of God in Christ Jesus.' We must learn to make the act of faith, and to know that no matter how bleak our surroundings, how dark the road, our God goes with us. That is the reality of the human situation and we must hold to it. We need to teach ourselves that God is the Light on our journey, we need to walk daily in the path of light.

Because the presence of God gives us hope and confidence, the prayer goes on '**I know my greatness**' – I think they are lovely words! We are great creatures, we are most marvellously made, and most wonderfully loved. As God cares so much for us, it is a tragedy if we have such a low estimate of ourselves. Each and every one of us has a greatness, for we are sons and daughters of God. If God made us and loves us, we need to learn to love ourselves. '**I know my greatness, Thou hast built me a throne within Thy heart.**' That is the reason for our greatness: we are loved by God. Again we need to affirm this every day – not once or twice but many times. I recognize in many Celtic prayers this ability to accept and affirm the presence. They did not talk *about* God as much as they talked *to* Him. God was not a theory but a person to be met with and to share with. I am in the heart of God – as the greater contains the lesser. Today there is much talk about the God in our hearts. That is good, but it is in danger of diminishing God. It is necessary to learn that we are in His heart, that in Him we live and move and have our being. Our feelings often will tell us lies and

suggest that God is far away, but it is not so: God is with us and about us.

Even when we sink into the deepest dark He is there, **I dwell safely within the circle of Thy care.** Time and again the Celt expressed this care of God in prayers called the *Caim*, prayers of encircling and protection. Even the fisherman braving one of the most dangerous seas in the world could say they did not fear because they were in the presence of the Father, Son and Holy Spirit. No matter what happened to them and their little boat, they were still in the care and love of God. This is something that many Christians of the twentieth century need to relearn.

'I cannot for a moment fall out of the everlasting arms.' When I think of these words, I see hands to uphold, and those hands that uphold bear the marks of the nails. I thank God for the coming down of Jesus into our lives, into the fullness of our experience. Not only did He come down to earth, He descended into all our tribulations, scorned and rejected, betrayed by a loved one, deserted and left alone, crucified, dead, buried, descended into hell – and all the hells of this world. He came down to lift us up, He came down to where we are that He could lift us to where He would have us be.

Every year I watch people being rescued from the causeway to Holy Island. Foolish people have misread the tide tables and tried to go off the Island when the tide is over the road. All who do this, do it because of something wrong in their estimates or attitude – but they are not left there for the tide to overwhelm them. If they are fortunate, RAF Boulmer sends out a Sea King helicopter, a winch man is lowered to where they are. He does not lecture them or tell them they deserve to be left, he puts his arms – and a harness – around them, and they are lifted up

to safety. Our God has promised that we shall not perish but have everlasting life – He will lift us up at the last, and more often if we will let Him.

Because we affirm that 'Underneath are the everlasting arms' we can extend our vision of ourselves and say **'I am on my way to glory'**. Again in a world that can be so debasing and self-destroying we need to know the reality that we are on our way to glory. When at theological college I had to write an essay on glory (it was like asking a sieve to carry water!), I went to the library and took out a theological word book and turned to 'glory' – it said simply 'see **God**'! Somehow I knew that was all that was needed – glory is to see God, not only at the end of time but in our midst, to affirm that it is God's world and He has not left His creation. We are not left as orphans as we are already children of God, we belong to Him and we are on our way towards Him. To be able to think and pray with this assurance is to walk in a path of light.

Here is the whole prayer by Alistair Maclean:

> **Though the dawn breaks cheerless on this isle today,**
> **my spirit walks upon a path of light.**
> **For I know my greatness.**
> **Thou hast built me a throne within Thy heart.**
> **I dwell safely within the circle of Thy care.**
> **I cannot for a moment fall out of the everlasting arms.**
> **I am on my way to Thy glory.**

BEFORE PRAYER

RUNE BEFORE PRAYER

I am bending my knee
In the eye of the Father who created me,
In the eye of the Son who purchased me,
In the eye of the Spirit who cleansed me,
    In friendship and affection.
Through Thine own Anointed One, O God,
Bestow upon us fullness in our need,
    Love towards God,
    The affection of God,
    The smile of God,
    The wisdom of God,
    The grace of God,
    The fear of God,
    And the will of God
To do on the world of the Three,
As angels and saints
Do in heaven;
    Each shade and light,
    Each day and night,
    Each time in kindness,
    Give then us Thy Spirit.

Carmina Gadelica 1, p. 3

PRAISING GOD

Let us praise God
at the beginning
and the end of time.
Who ever seeks Him out
He will not deny
nor refuse.

Black Book of Carmarthen

LORD, HAVE MERCY

God above us,
God before us,
God rules.
May the King of Heaven
give now the portion of mercy.

Black Book of Carmarthen

DEDICATION

'Tis God's will I would do,
My own will I would rein;
Would give to God His due,
From my own due refrain;
God's path I would pursue,
My own path would disdain.

Poems of the Western Highlanders, p. 59

FACING REALITY

Though the dawn breaks cheerless on this isle today,
my spirit walks upon a path of light.
For I know my greatness.
Thou hast built me a throne within Thy heart.
I dwell safely within the circle of Thy care.
I cannot for a moment fall out of the everlasting arms.
I am on my way to Thy glory.

Hebridean Altars, p. 55

RISING PRAYERS

THANKSGIVING

Thanks to Thee, O God, that I have risen to-day,
    To the rising of this life itself;
May it be to Thine own glory, O God of every gift,
    And to the glory of my soul likewise.

O great God, aid Thou my soul
    With the aiding of Thine own mercy;
Even as I clothe my body with wool,
    Cover Thou my soul with the shadow of Thy wing.

Help me to avoid every sin,
    And the source of every sin to forsake;
As the mist scatters on the crests of the hills,
    May each ill haze clear from my soul, O God.

Carmina Gadelica III, p. 31

PRAYER AT RISING

Bless to me, O God,
Each thing mine eye sees;
Bless to me, O God,
Each sound mine ear hears;
Bless to me, O God,
Each odour that goes into my nostrils;
Bless to me, O God,
Each taste that goes into my lips;
Each note that goes into my song,
Each ray that guides my way,
Each thing that I pursue,
Each lure that tempts my will,
The zeal that seeks my living soul,
The Three that seek my heart,
The zeal that seeks my living soul,
The Three that seek my heart.

Carmina Gadelica III, p. 33

THE DEER'S CRY (1)

I arise today
Through a mighty strength,
The invocation of the Trinity,
Through belief in the threeness,
Through confession of the oneness
Of the Creator of Creation.

I arise today
Through the strength of Christ's birth with His baptism,
Through the strength of His crucifixion with His burial,
Through the strength of His resurrection with His ascension,
Through the strength of His descent for the judgement of Doom.

I arise today
Through the strength of the love of the Cherubim,
In obedience of angels,
In the service of archangels,
In the hope of resurrection to meet with reward,
In prayers of patriarchs,
In predictions of prophets,
In preaching of apostles,
In faith of confessors,
In innocence of holy virgins,
In deeds of righteous men.

Selections from Ancient Irish Poetry, p. 25

THE DEER'S CRY (2)

I arise today
Through the strength of heaven:
Light of sun,
Radiance of moon,
Splendour of fire,
Speed of lightning,
Swiftness of wind,
Depth of sea,
Stability of earth,
Firmess of rock.

I arise today
Through God's strength to pilot me:
God's might to uphold me,
God's wisdom to guide me,
God's eye to look before,
God's ear to hear me,
God's word to speak for me,
God's hand to guard me,
God's way to lie before me,
God's shield to protect me,
God's host to save me
From snares of devils,
From temptation of vices,
From every one who shall wish me ill,

Afar and near,
Alone and in a multitude.

Selections from Ancient Irish Poetry, pp. 25–6

SUNRISE

King of the brightness and of the sun,
You alone know the reason for our being,
Be with us every day,
Be with us every night,
Be with us every night and day
Be with us every day and night.

Saltair, p. 8

ON RISING

I rise with God,
May God rise with me.
The hand of God about me
In my waking and in my sleeping and in my rising up.

Saltair, p. 8

MORNING PRAYERS

MORNING PRAYER

I am giving Thee worship with my whole life,
    I am giving Thee assent with my whole power,
I am giving Thee praise with my whole tongue,
    I am giving Thee honour with my whole utterance.

I am giving Thee reverence with my whole understanding,
    I am giving Thee offering with my whole thought,
I am giving Thee praise with my whole fervour,
    I am giving Thee humility in the blood of the Lamb.

I am giving Thee love with my whole devotion,
    I am giving Thee kneeling with my whole desire,
I am giving Thee love with my whole heart,
    I am giving Thee affection with my whole sense;
I am giving Thee my existence with my whole mind,
    I am giving Thee my soul, O God of all gods.

Carmina Gadelica III, p. 45

MORNING PRAYER

Thou has brought me up from last night
To the gracious light of this day,
Great joy to provide for my soul,
And to do excelling good to me.

Thanks be to Thee, Jesus Christ,
    For the many gifts Thou hast bestowed on me,
Each day and night, each sea and land,
    Each weather fair, each calm, each wild.

Carmina Gadelica iii, pp. 43–5

PRAYER AT DRESSING

Bless to me, O God,
    My soul and my body;
Bless to me, O God,
    My belief and my condition;

Bless to me, O God,
    My heart and my speech,
And bless to me, O God,
    The handling of my hand;

Strength and busyness of morning,
    Habit and temper of modesty,
    Force and wisdom of thought,
    And Thine own path, O God of virtues,
Till I go to sleep this night;

Thine own path, O God of virtues
Till I go to sleep this night.

Carmina Gadelica III, p. 27

MORNING PRAYER

Thanks be to Thee, Jesus Christ,
Who brought'st me up from last night,
To the gladsome light of this day,
To win everlasting life for my soul,
Through the blood Thou didst shed for me.

Praise be to Thee, O God, for ever,
For the blessings Thou didst bestow on me –
My food, my speech, my work, my health,

*   *   *   *

And I beseech Thee
To shield me from sin,
To shield me from ill,
To sain me this night,
And I low and poor,
O God of the poor!
O Christ of the wounds!
Give me wisdom along with Thy grace.

May the Holy One claim me,
And protect me on sea and on land,
And lead me on from step to step,
To the peace of the Everlasting City,
    The peace of the Everlasting City!

Carmina Gadelica I, p. 97

THE GUIDING LIGHT OF ETERNITY

O God, who broughtst me from the rest of last night
Unto the joyous light of this day,
Be Thou bringing me from the new light of this day
Unto the guiding light of eternity.
    Oh! from the new light of this day
    Unto the guiding light of eternity.

Carmina Gadelica 1, p. 33

AFFIRMATIONS

THE SECRET OF GENTLENESS

There is no secret –
only – only I am always at His feet,
and He is always in my heart.

Hebridean Altars, p. 77

FLAME OF LOVE

Would that me also, wretched though I be, yet His poor servant, He might deign so to arouse from the sleep of idleness, so to kindle with that fire of divine love, that the flame of His love, the longing of His so great charity, would mount above the stars, and the divine fire would ever burn within me! Would that I had the tinder to foster, feed, and keep alight that fire unceasingly, and nourish that flame, which knows no quenching and knows all increase!

Sancti Columbani Opera, pp. 113–15

THOUGHTS

God's will would I do,
My own will bridle;

God's due I would give,
My own due yield;

God's path would I travel,
My own path refuse;

Christ's death would I ponder,
My own death remember,

Christ's agony would I meditate,
My love to God make warmer ...

Carmina Gadelica III, p. 51

JESU WHO OUGHT TO BE PRAISED

It were as easy for Jesu
To renew the withered tree
As to wither the new
Were it His will so to do.
    Jesu! Jesu! Jesu!
    Jesu! meet it were to praise Him.

There is no plant in the ground
But is full of His virtue,
There is no form in the strand
But is full of His blessing.
    Jesu! Jesu! Jesu!
    Jesu! meet it were to praise Him.

There is no life in the sea,
There is no creature in the river,
There is naught in the firmament,
But proclaims His goodness.
    Jesu! Jesu! Jesu!
    Jesu! meet it were to praise Him.

There is no bird on the wing,
There is no star in the sky,
There is nothing beneath the sun,
But proclaims His goodness.
    Jesu! Jesu! Jesu!
    Jesu! meet it were to praise Him.

Carmina Gadelica 1, pp. 39–41

HEY THE GIFT, HO THE GIFT

Hey the Gift, ho the Gift,
Hey the Gift, on the living.

Son of the dawn, Son of the clouds,
Son of the planet, Son of the star,
   Hey the Gift, etc.

Son of the rain, Son of the dew,
Son of the welkin, Son of the sky,
   Hey the Gift, etc.

Son of the flame, son of the light,
Son of the sphere, Son of the globe,
   Hey the Gift, etc.

Son of the elements, Son of the heavens,
Son of the moon, Son of the sun,
   Hey the Gift, etc.

Son of Mary of the God-mind,
And the Son of God first of all news,
   Hey the Gift, etc.

Carmina Gadelica 1, p. 141

MORNING PRAYER

I believe, O God of all gods,
    That Thou art the eternal Father of life;
I believe, O God of all gods,
    That Thou art the eternal Father of love.

I believe, O God of all gods,
    That Thou art the eternal Father of the saints;
I believe, O God of all gods,
    That Thou art the eternal Father of each one.

I believe, O God of all gods,
    That Thou art the eternal Father of mankind;
I believe, O God of all gods,
    That Thou art the eternal Father of the world.

I believe, O Lord and God of the peoples,
That Thou art the creator of the high heavens,
That Thou art the creator of the skies above,
That Thou art the creator of the oceans below.

I believe, O Lord and God of the peoples,
    That Thou art He Who created my soul and set its warp,

Who created my body from dust and from ashes,
    Who gave to my body breath, and to my body its possession.

Father, bless to me my body,
Father, bless to me my soul,
Father, bless to me my life,
Father, bless to me my belief.

Carmina Gadelica III, pp. 41–3

GOD'S AID

God to enfold me,
God to surround me,
God in my speaking,
God in my thinking.

God in my sleeping,
God in my waking,
God in my watching,
God in my hoping.

God in my life,
God in my lips,
God in my soul,
God in my heart.

God in my sufficing,
God in my slumber,
God in mine ever-living soul,
God in mine eternity.

Carmina Gadelica III, p. 53

FRAGMENT

In the love of God,
In the affection of God,
In the will of God,
In the eye of God,
In the purpose of God,
In the charge of God.

Carmina Gadelica III, p. 87

PEACE

Peace between neighbours,
Peace between kindred,
Peace between lovers,
    In the love of the King of life.

Peace between person and person,
Peace between wife and husband,
Peace between woman and children,
The peace of Christ above all peace.

Bless, O Christ, my face,
    Let my face bless every thing;
Bless, O Christ, mine eye,
    Let mine eye bless all it sees.

Carmina Gadelica III, p. 267

GOD WITH ME

God be with me
In this, Thy day,
Every day,
And every way,
With me and for me,
In this Thy day.

Old Celtic Prayer, in *Hebridean Altars*, p. 62

LOVE LIGHTING

God, kindle Thou my heart within
A love flame to my neighbour-kin,
To foe, to friend, to blood-near all,
To brave, to knave, and to the thrall.
O Son of loveliest Mary, Thou,
Before Thee with this prayer I bow:
Kindle Thou in my heart within
A love to Thee and neighbour-kin.

Hebridean Altars, p. 48

SERENITY

I am serene because I know Thou lovest me.
Because Thou lovest me, naught can move me from Thy peace.
Because Thou lovest me, I am as one to whom all good has come.

Hebridean Altars, p. 99

GOD OF ALL

Our God is the God of all,
The God of heaven and earth,
Of the sea and of the rivers;
The God of the sun and of the moon and of all the stars;
The God of the lofty mountains
And of the lowly valleys.
He has His dwelling around heaven and earth,
And sea, and all that in them is.
He inspires all,
He gives life to all,
He dominates all,
He supports all.
He lights the light of the sun.
He furnishes the light of the night.
He has made springs in dry land …
He is the God of heaven and earth,
Of sea and rivers,
Of sun, moon and stars,
Of the lofty mountain and the lowly valley,
The God above heaven,
And in heaven,
And under heaven.

St Patrick

HOPE IN GOD

Christ is the world's redeemer,
The lover of the pure,
The fount of heavenly wisdom,
Our trust and hope secure;
The armour of his soldiers,
The Lord of earth and sky;
Our health while we are living,
Our life when we shall die.

St Patrick

GREETINGS

Glorious God,
Greetings,
May church and chancel
Bless You,
May highland and lowland
Bless You,
May the three fountains
Bless You,
Two above the wind,
One above the earth;
May darkness and daylight
Bless You …

I bless you,
Lord of majesty,
Glorious God,
Greetings.

Black Book of Carmarthen

PROTECTION AND HEALING

A GENERAL SUPPLICATION

God, listen to my prayer,
Bend to me Thine ear,
Let my supplications and my prayers
Ascend to Thee upwards,
Come, Thou King of Glory,
To protect me down,
Thou King of Life and mercy
With the aid of the Lamb,
Thou Son of Mary Virgin
To protect me with power,
Thou Son of the lovely Mary
Of purest fairest beauty.

Carmina Gadelica 1, p. 13

GOD WITH ME LYING DOWN

God with me lying down,
God with me rising up,
God with me in each ray of light,
Nor I a ray of joy without Him,
    Nor one ray without Him.

Christ with me sleeping,
Christ with me waking,
Christ with me watching,
Every day and night,
    Each day and night.

God with me protecting,
The Lord with me directing,
The Spirit with me strengthening;
For ever and for evermore,
    Ever and evermore, Amen.
    Chief of chiefs, Amen.

Carmina Gadelica 1, p. 5

THE SOUL PLAINT

O Jesu! to-night,
Thou Shepherd of the poor,
Thou sinless person
Who didst suffer full sore,
By ban of the wicked,
And wast crucified.

Save me from evil,
Save me from harm,
Save Thou my body,
Sanctify me to-night,
O Jesu! to-night,
Nor leave me.

Endow me with strength,
Thou Herdsman of might,
Guide me aright,
Guide me in Thy strength,
O Jesu! in Thy strength
Preserve me.

Carmina Gadelica 1, p. 71

PROTECTION

I am beseeching Thee
To keep me from ill,
To keep me from hurt,
To keep me from harm;

To keep me from mischance,
To keep me from grief,
To keep me this night
    In the nearness of Thy love.

May God shield me,
    May God fill me,
    May God keep me,
    May God watch me.

May God bring me
    To the land of peace,
    To the country of the King,
    To the peace of eternity.

Praise to the Father,
    Praise to the Son,
    Praise to the Spirit
    The Three in One.

Carmina Gadelica III, pp. 45–7

SUPPLICATION

O Being of life!
O Being of peace!
O Being of time!
    O Being of eternity!
    O Being of eternity!

Keep me in good means,
    Keep me in good intent,
Keep me in good estate,
    Better than I know to ask,
    Better than I know to ask!

Shepherd me this day,
    Relieve my distress,
Enfold me this night,
    Pour upon me Thy grace,
    Pour upon me Thy grace!

Guard for me my speech,
    Strengthen for me my love,
Illume for me the stream,
    Succour Thou me in death,
    Succour Thou me in death!

Carmina Gadelica III, p. 55

THOU, MY SOUL'S HEALER

Thou, my soul's Healer,
Keep me at even,
Keep me at morning,
Keep me at noon,
On rough course faring;
Help and safeguard
My means this night.
  I am tired, astray, and stumbling,
  Shield Thou me from snare and sin.

Carmina Gadelica III, p. 85

PRAYER

The Son of God be shielding me from harm,
The Son of God be shielding me from ill,
The Son of God be shielding me from mishap,
The Son of God be shielding me this night.

The Son of God be shielding me with might,
The Son of God be shielding me with power;
Each one who is dealing with me aright,
   So may God deal with his soul.

Carmina Gadelica III, pp. 99–101

ENCOMPASSING

The compassing of God be on thee,
    The compassing of the God of life.

The compassing of Christ be on thee,
    The compassing of the Christ of love.

The compassing of the Spirit be on thee,
    The compassing of the Spirit of Grace.

The compassing of the Three be on thee,
    The compassing of the Three preserve thee,
    The compassing of the Three preserve thee.

Carmina Gadelica III, p. 105

PETITION

Be Thou a smooth way before me,
Be Thou a guiding star above me,
Be Thou a keen eye behind me,
This day, this night, for ever.

Carmina Gadelica III, p. 171

PROTECTION

Deliver us, O Lord, from evil.
O Lord Jesu Christ, keep us always in every good work.
O God, the fountain and author of all good things,
Empty us of vices, and fill us with good virtues.

The Reliques of Ancient Scottish Devotions, p. 21

THE SUN OF GOD

The eye of the great God,
The eye of the God of glory,
The eye of the King of hosts,
The eye of the King of the living,
    Pouring upon us
    At each time and season,
    Pouring upon us
    Gently and generously.

Carmina Gadelica III, p. 306

PRAYER

My God and my Chief,
    I seek to Thee in the morning,
My God and my Chief,
    I seek to Thee this night.
I am giving Thee my mind,
    I am giving Thee my will,
I am giving Thee my wish,
    My soul everlasting and my body.

Mayest Thou be chieftain over me,
    Mayest Thou be master unto me,
Mayest Thou be shepherd over me,
    Mayest Thou be guardian unto me,
Mayest Thou be herdsman over me,
    Mayest Thou be guide unto me,
Mayest Thou be with me, O Chief of chiefs,
    Father everlasting and God of the heavens.

Carmina Gadelica III, p. 347

THE PROTECTION OF CHRIST

Christ as a light
Illumine and guide me!
Christ as a shield overshadow and cover me!
Christ be under me! Christ be over me!
Christ be beside me,
On left hand and right!
Christ be before me, behind me, about me!
Christ, this day, be within and without me!

St Patrick

THE PROTECTING GOD

Lord be with us this day,
Within us to purify us;
Above us to draw us up;
Beneath us to sustain us;
Before us to lead us;
Behind us to restrain us;
Around us to protect us.

St Patrick

PRAYER OF ST MERYADOC

Lord, who made sea and land,
Always give me aid,
And guide my life here
In the way of truth.
Lord Jesus, look on me,
And grant me Thy unfailing grace.
Every hour, Jesus, it is my desire
In the world to please you.

From *Bewnans Meryasek*, quoted in
The Saints of Cornwall, p. 26

PROTECTION

Jesu MacMary, at dawn-tide, the flowing
Jesu MacMary, at ebb-tide, the going:
When our first breath awakes,
Life's day when darkness takes,
Merciful God of all, mercy bestowing,
With us and for us be,
Merciful Deity,
Amen, eternally.

Poems of the Western Highlanders, p. 268

TO JESUS

God to guide me, God to teach me, God to counsel me,
God to protect me wherever sin may be.
Loving Jesus, who received grace from your Father,
lead me, wherever I may be, through the gap of safety.

Saltair, p. 8

DEDICATION AND WORK

BLESSING OF HOUSE

God bless the house,
From site to stay,
From beam to wall,
From end to end,
From ridge to basement,
From balk to roof-tree,
From found to summit,
    Found and summit.

Carmina Gadelica 1, p. 105

SEA PRAYER

HELMSMAN	Blest be the boat.
CREW	God the Father bless her.
HELMSMAN	Blest be the boat.
CREW	God the Son bless her.
HELMSMAN	Blest be the boat.
CREW	God the Spirit bless her.
ALL	God the Father, God the Son, God the Spirit, Bless the boat.
HELMSMAN	What can befall you And God the Father with you?
CREW	No harm can befall us.
HELMSMAN	What can befall you And God the Son with you?
CREW	No harm can befall us.
HELMSMAN	What can befall you And God the Spirit with you?
CREW	No harm can befall us.
ALL	God the Father, God the Son, God the Spirit, With us eternally.

HELMSMAN	What can cause you anxiety
	And the God of the elements over you?
CREW	No anxiety can be ours.
HELMSMAN	What can cause you anxiety
	And the King of the elements over you?
CREW	No anxiety can be ours.
HELMSMAN	What can cause you anxiety
	And the Spirit of the elements over you?
CREW	No anxiety can be ours.
ALL	The God of the elements,
	The King of the elements,
	The Spirit of the elements,
	Close over us,
	Ever eternally.

Carmina Gadelica 1, pp. 333–5

PRAYER

Father, bless me in my body,
    Father, bless me in my soul;
Father, bless me this night
    In my body and in my soul.

Father, bless me in my life,
    Father, bless me in my creed;
Father, bless me in my tie
    To my life and to my creed.

Father, sanctify me in my speech,
    Father, sanctify me in my heart;
Father, sanctify to me every whit
    In my speech and in my heart.

Carmina Gadelica III, p. 349

FOR LIGHT

Lord grant me,
I pray Thee in the name of Jesus Christ the Son, my God,
That love which knows no fall
So that my lamp may feel thy kindling touch
And know no quenching;
May burn for me
And for others may give light.

Columbanus

BE THOU MY VISION

Be Thou my Vision, O Lord of my heart:
Naught is all else to me, save that Thou art,
Thou my best thought, by day and by night,
Waking or sleeping, Thy presence my light.

Be Thou my Wisdom, Thou my true Word;
I ever with Thee, Thou with me Lord.
Thou my great Father, I Thy dear son,
Thou in me dwelling, I with Thee one.

Be Thou my breastplate, my sword for the fight;
Be Thou my whole armour, be Thou my true might;
Be Thou my soul's shelter, be Thou my strong tower:
O raise Thou me heavenward, great Power of my power.

Riches I heed not, nor man's empty praise:
Be Thou mine inheritance now and always;
Be Thou and Thou only the first in my heart;
O Sovereign of heaven, my treasure Thou art.

High King of heaven, Thou heaven's bright Sun,
O grant me its joys after vic'try is won;
Great Heart of mine own heart, whatever befall,
Still be Thou my vision, O Ruler of all.

The Poem Book of the Gael, pp. 119–20

CHRIST IN OTHERS

Christ the lowly and meek,
Christ the all powerful,
Be in the heart of each to whom I speak,
In the mouth of each who speaks to me,
In all who draw near me,
Or see me, or hear me!

St Patrick

HOSPITALITY

O King of the stars!
Whether my house be dark or bright,
Never shall it be closed to any one,
Lest Christ close his House against me.

If there be a guest in your house
And you conceal aught from him
'Tis not the guest that will be without it,
But Jesus, Mary's Son.

Selections from Ancient Irish Poetry, p. 100

DEDICATION

Rule this heart of mine,
O dread God of the elements,
That Thou mayest be my love,
That I may do Thy will.

Selections from Ancient Irish Poetry, p. 36

TO BE WITH GOD

Almighty God,
Father, Son and Holy Ghost,
To me the least of saints,
To me allow that I may keep a door in Paradise.
That I may keep even the smallest door,
The farthest, darkest, coldest door,
The door that is least used, the stiffest door.
If only it be in Thine house, O God,
That I can see Thy glory even afar,
And hear Thy voice,
And know that I am with Thee, O God.

St Columba

BALANCED LIFE

That I might bless the Lord
Who conserves all,
Heaven with its countless bright orders,
Land, strand and flood,
That I might search all the books
That would be good for my soul,
At times kneeling to beloved heaven,
At times at psalm singing:
At times contemplating the king of heaven,
Holy the chief,
At times at work without compulsion,
This would be delightful.
At times picking kelp from the rocks;
At times fishing;
At times giving food to the poor;
At times in a solitary cell,
The best advice to me has been granted.

St Columba

THE LOVE LIGHT OF CHRIST

O Lord, give us, we beseech Thee,
In the Name of Jesus Christ Thy Son our Lord,
That love which can never cease,
That will kindle our lamps but not extinguish them,
That they may burn in us and enlighten others.

Do Thou O Christ, our dearest Saviour,
Thyself kindle our lamps,
That they may evermore shine in Thy temple
And receive unquenchable light from Thee
That will enlighten our darkness
And lessen the darkness of the world.

St Columba

FAITH AND WORKS

'The tempests howl, the storms dismay,
But manly strength can win the day.
Heave, lads, and let the echoes ring

For clouds and squalls will soon pass on,
And victory lie with work well done
Heave, lads, and let the echoes ring ...

The King of virtues vowed a prize
For him who wins, for him who tries,
Think, lads, of Christ and echo him.'

Columbanus In His Own Words, pp. 98–9

PRAYER BEFORE WORK

Be in my heart, O Jesus, to fix my thoughts on You;
Be in my heart, O Jesus, to give me sorrow for my sin;
Be in my heart, O Jesus, to fill me with devotion;
O Jesus, loving God, may You never part from me.

Without You, O Jesus, my thoughts can never please me;
Without You, O Jesus, I cannot write or speak;
Without You, O Jesus, all I do is useless;
O Jesus, loving God, stand before me and behind me.

Saltair, p. 14

PENITENCE

I confess to You, great God all-powerful,
My sins, my faults beyond number,
From the day of my christening to the day of my wake,
Through the thoughts of my heart,
Through the sight of my eyes,
Through the hearing of my ears,
Through the words of my mouth,
Through the course of my journey,
Through all that I have said that was untrue,
Through all that I have promised and not fulfilled,
Through all that I have done to break Your laws
And Your holy commandments.
I now ask for Your forgiveness
In the gentle name of Jesus,
For fear I may have never asked it before
In the way a sinner like me should ask it,
And for fear I may not live to ask it again,
In the name of the Father and of the Son and of the Holy Spirit.

Saltair, p. 26

CONFESSION

Many and vast are my sins in their mass,
Through my heart and round about it like a net or a breast-plate;
O King that cannot be numbered;
Despoil me of them, O God;
Break, smite and war against them;
Ravage, bend and wither them;
Take away, repel, destroy them;
Arise, scatter, defeat them;
See, repress, waste them;
Torture, divide and purify them;
Tear, expel and raze them;
Remove, scatter and cleave them;
Subdue, exhaust and lay them low.

Irish Litanies, p. 9

LIGHT WITHIN

Grant to me, I beseech You O my God,
In the name of Jesus your Son,
The love which never fails,
That my light may shine,
Warming my own heart
And enlightening others.

Columbanus

JOURNEYING

THE PATH I WALK

The path I walk, Christ walks it.
May the land in which I am be without sorrow.
May the Trinity protect me wherever I stay,
Father, Son and Holy Spirit.
Bright angels walk with me – dear presence – in every dealing.
In every dealing I pray them that no one's poison may reach me.
The ninefold people of heaven of holy cloud, the tenth force of the stout
    earth.
Favourable company, they come with me, so that the Lord may not be
    angry with me.
May I arrive at every place, may I return home, may the way in which I
    spend be a way without loss.
May every path before me be smooth, man, woman and child welcome
    me.
A truly good journey! Well does the fair Lord show us a course, a path.

Attributed to St Columba
Celtic Christian Spirituality, p. 38

THE ROAD OF BRIGHTNESS

Be with me and for me, dear Lord,
As I walk upon the road of brightness
That runs between earth and Thy glory.

From the Island of Coll
Hebridean Altars, p. 91

THE PATH OF RIGHT

My walk this day with God,
My walk this day with Christ,
My walk this day with Spirit,
    The Threefold all kindly:
    Hò! hò! hò! the Threefold all-kindly.

My shielding this day from ill,
My shielding this night from harm,
Hò! Hò! both my soul and my body,
    Be by Father, by Son, by Holy Spirit:
    By Father, by Son, by Holy Spirit.

Be the Father shielding me,
Be the Son shielding me,
Be the Spirit shielding me,
    As Three and as One:
    Hò! hò! hò! as Three and as One.

Carmina Gadelica III, p. 49

THE GUARDIAN ANGEL

Be thou a bright flame before me,
Be thou a guiding star above me,
Be thou a smooth path below me,
And be a kindly shepherd behind me,
To-day, to-night, and for ever.

Carmina Gadelica I, p. 49

THE JOURNEY BLESSING

Bless to me, O God,
    The earth beneath my foot,
Bless to me, O God,
    The path whereon I go;
Bless to me, O God,
    The thing of my desire;
    Thou Evermore of evermore,
    Bless Thou to me my rest.

Bless to me the thing
    Whereon is set my mind,
Bless to me the thing
    Whereon is set my love;
Bless to me the thing
    Whereon is set my hope;
    O Thou King of kings,
    Bless Thou to me mine eye!

Carmina Gadelica III, p. 181

THE PILGRIMS' AIDING

God be with thee in every pass,
Jesus be with thee on every hill,
Spirit be with thee on every stream,
    Headland and ridge and lawn;

Each sea and land, each moor and meadow,
Each lying down, each rising up,
In the trough of the waves, on the crest of the billows,
    Each step of the journey thou goest.

Carmina Gadelica III, p. 195

CHARM FOR FEAR BY NIGHT

God before me, God behind me,
God above me, God below me;
I on the path of God,
God upon my track.

Carmina Gadelica III, p. 319

GOD GUIDE ME

God guide me with Thy wisdom,
God chastise me with Thy justice,
God help me with Thy mercy,
God protect me with Thy strength.

God fill me with Thy fullness,
God shield me with Thy shade,
God fill me with Thy grace,
For the sake of Thine Anointed Son.

Jesu Christ of the seed of David,
Visiting One of the Temple,
Sacrificial Lamb of the Garden,
Who died for me.

Carmina Gadelica 1, p. 65

CONFIDENCE IN GOD

Alone with none but Thee, my God,
I journey on my way.
What need I fear, when Thou art near,
O King of night and day?
More safe I am within Thy hand
Than if a host did round me stand.

St Columba

LITANIES

JESU, THOU SON OF MARY

Jesu, Thou Son of Mary,
Have mercy on us,
    Amen.
Jesu, Thou Son of Mary,
Make peace with us,
    Amen.
Oh, with us and for us
Where we shall longest be,
    Amen.
Be about the morning of our course,
Be about the close of life,
    Amen.
Be at the dawning of our life,
And oh! at the dark'ning of our day,
    Amen.
Be for us and with us,
Merciful God of all,
    Amen.
Consecrate us
Condition and lot,
Thou King of kings,
Thou God of all,
    Amen.

Consecrate us
Rights and means,
Thou King of kings,
Thou God of all,
    Amen.
Heart and body,
Thou King of kings,
Thou God of all,
    Amen.
Each heart and body,
Each day to Thyself,
Each night accordingly,
Thou King of kings,
Thou God of all,
    Amen.

Carmina Gadelica I, p. 19

LITANY

O God above all gods,
O King above all kings,
O Man above men,
    Forgive.
O World above worlds,
O Power above powers,
O Love above loves,
    Forgive.
O Cause above causes,
O Fortress above fortresses,
O Angel above angels,
    Forgive.

Irish Litany

TO THE ETERNAL FATHER

Have mercy on us, O God,
Father almighty,
God most high,
God of hosts,
Lord of the world,
God invisible,
God incorruptible,
God immortal,
God all merciful,
God all perfect,
Have mercy on us.

God of earth,
God of fire,
God of fresh waters,
God of great winds,
God of shining stars,
God who made the world,
God of many tongues,
God of the nations,
God of golden goodness,
Heavenly Father,
have mercy on us.

Saltair, p. 62

LITANY OF CONFESSION

O Father, O Son, O Holy Spirit,
    Forgive me my sins.
O only begotten Son of the heavenly Father
    Forgive.
O one God, O true God, O chief God,
O God of one substance,
O God only mighty, in three Persons, truly pitiful,
    Forgive.
O God rewarder, forgiving, loving, pre-eminent,
Immense, vast mysterious,
    Forgive.
O God above all gods,
O King above all kings,
O Man above all men,
    Forgive.
O World above all worlds,
O Power above all powers,
O Love above all loves,
    Forgive.
O Cause above all causes,
O Fortress above all fortresses,
O Angel above all angels,
    Forgive.

Irish Litanies, p. 3

LITANY OF JESUS

O holy Jesu:
O gentle friend:
O Morning Star:
O mid-day Sun adorned;
O brilliant flame of the righteous and of righteousness,
And of everlasting life, and of eternity;
O fountain ever-new, ever-living, ever-lasting;
O heart's Desire of patriarchs;
O Longing of prophets:
O Master of apostles and disciples;
O Giver of the Law;
O Prince of the New Testament;
O Judge of doom;
O Son of the merciful Father without mother in heaven;
O Son of the true virgin maid, Mary, without father on earth;
O true and loving brother.

Irish Litanies, p. 41

LITANY TO THE TRINITY (1)

Have mercy upon us, O God the Father Almighty:
O God of hosts,
O high God,
O Lord of the world,
O ineffable God,
O Creator of the Elements,
O invisible God,
O incorporeal God,
O God beyond all judgement,
O immeasurable God,
O impassible God,
O incorruptible God,
O immortal God,
O immovable God,
O eternal God,
O perfect God,
O merciful God,
O wondrous God,
O dreadful God,
O God of the earth,
O God of fire,
O God of the excellent waters,
O God of the tempestuous and rushing air,
O God of the many languages round the circuit of the earth,
O God of the waves from the bottomless house of the ocean,

O God of the constellations and all the bright stars,
O God who didst fashion the mass, and didst inaugurate day and night,
O God who didst rule over hell, and its rabble host,
O God who dost govern with archangels,
O golden good,
O heavenly Father who art in heaven,
    Have mercy upon us.

Irish Litanies, p. 79

LITANY TO THE TRINITY (2)

Have mercy upon us, O Almighty God, Jesus Christ, Son of the living God,
O Son twice born,
O only begotten of God the Father,
O first born of the Virgin Mary,
O Son of David,
O Son of Abraham,
O beginning of all things,
O completion of the world,
O Word of God,
O way to the heavenly kingdom,
O Life of all things,
O everlasting Righteousness,
O Image, O Likeness, O Form of God the Father,
O Arm of God,
O Hand of God,
O Might of God,
O Right-hand of God,
O true Knowledge,
O true Light of love, that lighteneth every darkness,
O guiding Light,
O Sun of righteousness.
O Morning star,
O Brightness of Deity,
O Radiance of the eternal brightness …
Have mercy upon us.

Irish Litanies, p. 81

LITANY TO THE TRINITY (3)

Have mercy upon us, O God Almighty, O Holy Spirit;
O Spirit that art highest of all spirits,
O Finger of God,
O Protection of Christians,
O Comforter of the sorrowful,
O Clement one,
O merciful Intercessor,
O Imparter of true wisdom,
O Author of the Holy Scriptures,
O Ruler of speech,
O septiform Spirit,
O Spirit of wisdom,
O Spirit of understanding,
O Spirit of counsel,
O Spirit of strength,
O Spirit of knowledge,
O Spirit of affection,
O Spirit of fear,
O Spirit of love,
O Spirit of grace,
O Spirit from whom is ordered every lofty thing,
O Spirit that burnest up guilt,
O Spirit that washest sins,
O Holy Spirit that rulest all created things, visible and invisible
Have mercy upon us.

Irish Litanies, pp. 83–5

SLEEP

A PRAYER

O God,
In my deeds,
In my words,
In my wishes,
In my reason,
And in the fulfilling of my desires,
In my sleep,
In my dreams,
In my repose,
In my thoughts,
In my heart and soul always …

Carmina Gadelica I, p. 27

SLEEPING PRAYER

I am placing my soul and my body
On Thy sanctuary this night, O God,
On Thy sanctuary, O Jesus Christ,
On Thy sanctuary, O Spirit of perfect truth,
    The Three who would defend my cause,
    Nor turn Their backs upon me.

Thou, Father, who art kind and just,
Thou, Son, who didst overcome death,
Thou, Holy Spirit of power,
Be keeping me this night from harm;
    The Three who would justify me
    Keeping me this night and always.

Carmina Gadelica I, p. 73

106

I LIE DOWN THIS NIGHT

I lie down this night with God,
    And God will lie down with me;
I lie down this night with Christ,
    And Christ will lie down with me;
I lie down this night with the Spirit,
    And the Spirit will lie down with me;
God and Christ and the Spirit
    Be lying down with me.

Carmina Gadelica III, p. 333

REPOSE OF SLEEP

O God of life, darken not to me Thy light,
O God of life, close not to me Thy joy,
O God of life, shut not to me Thy door,
    O God of life, refuse not to me Thy mercy,
    O God of life, quench Thou to me Thy wrath,
    And O God of life, crown Thou to me Thy gladness,
O God of life, crown Thou to me Thy gladness.

Carmina Gadelica III, p. 343

THE SOUL PLAINT

O Jesu! to-night,
Thou Shepherd of the poor,
Thou sinless person
Who didst suffer full sore,
By ban of the wicked,
And wast crucified.

Save me from evil,
Save me from harm,
Save Thou my body,
Sanctify me to-night,
O Jesu! to-night,
Nor leave me.

Endow me with strength,
Thou Herdsman of might,
Guide me aright,
Guide me in Thy strength,
O Jesu! in Thy strength
Preserve me.

Carmina Gadelica 1, p. 71

TO THE TRINITY

PRAISE BEYOND WORDS

1. Almighty Creator, thou hast made …

2. The world cannot express in song bright and melodious, even
   though the grass and the trees should sing, all thy glories
   (miracles, riches), O true Lord!

3. The Father has wrought [such a multitude] of wonders in this
   world that it is difficult to find an equal number. Letters
   cannot contain it, letters cannot express it.

* * *

5. He who made the wonder of the world, will save us, has saved
   us. It is not too great toil to praise the Trinity.

6. Purely, without blemish, in the great assembly, let us extol …

7. Purely, humbly, in skilful verse, I should love to give praise to
   the Trinity, according to the greatness of his power.

The Beginnings of Welsh Poetry, p. 102

THE THREE

In name of Father,
In name of Son,
In name of Spirit,
    Three in One:

Father cherish me,
Son cherish me,
Spirit cherish me,
    Three all-kindly.

God make me holy,
Christ make me holy,
Spirit make me holy,
    Three all-holy.

Three aid my hope,
Three aid my love,
Three aid my eye,
    And my knee from stumbling,
    My knee from stumbling.

Carmina Gadelica III, p. 63

THE THREE

The Three Who are over me,
The Three Who are below me,
The Three Who are above me here,
The Three Who are above me yonder,
The Three Who are in the earth,
The Three Who are in the air,
The Three Who are in the heaven,
  The Three Who are in the great pouring sea.

Carmina Gadelica III, p. 93

COME I THIS DAY

Come I this day to the Father,
Come I this day to the Son,
Come I to the Holy Spirit powerful;
Come I this day with God,
Come I this day with Christ,
Come I this day with the Spirit of kindly balm.

God, and Spirit, and Jesus,
From the crown of my head
To the soles of my feet;
Come I with my reputation,
Come I with my testimony,
Come I to thee, Jesu –
    Jesu, shelter me.

Carmina Gadelica 1, p. 69

THE THREE EVERYWHERE

The Three who are over my head,
The Three who are under my tread,
The Three who are over me here,
The Three who are over me there,
The Three who are in the earth near,
The Three who are up in the air,
The Three who in heaven do dwell,
The Three in the great ocean swell,
Pervading Three, O be with me.

Poems of the Western Highlanders, p. 361

PRAISE TO THE TRINITY

I praise the threefold
Trinity as God,
Who is one and three,
A single power in unity.
His attributes a single mystery,
One God to praise,
Great King, I praise you,
Great your glory,
Your praise is true:
I am the one who praises you:
Poetry's welfare
Is in Elohim's care.
Hail to you O Christ;
Father, Son
And Holy Ghost:
Our Adonai.

Celtic Christian Spirituality, p. 30

PRAYER TO THE TRINITY

Teach me O Trinity,
All men sing praise to Thee
Let me not backward be,
Teach me O Trinity.

Come Thou and dwell within me,
Lord of the holy race;
Make here Thy resting place,
Hear me O Trinity.

That I Thy love may prove,
Teach Thou my heart and hand,
Even at Thy command
Swiftly to move.

Like a rotting tree,
Is this vile heart of me;
Let me Thy healing see,
Help me O Trinity.

The Poem Book of the Gael, pp. 157–8

HYMN OF PRAISE

Blessing and brightness,
Wisdom and thanksgiving,
Great power and might
To the King who rules over all.

Glory and honour and goodwill,
Praise and the sublime song of minstrels,
Overflowing love from every heart
To the King of heaven and earth.

To the chosen Trinity has been joined
Before all, after all, universal
Blessing and everlasting blessing,
Blessing everlasting and blessing.

Celtic Christian Spirituality, p. 29

THE ETERNAL

As it was,
As it is,
As it shall be evermore,
God of grace,
God in Trinity!
With the ebb, with the flow,
Ever it is so,
God of grace,
O Trinity,
With the ebb and flow.

Poems of the Western Highlanders, pp. 216–7

BLESSINGS

BLESSING

Bless ourselves and our children,
Bless every one who shall come from our loins,
Bless him whose name we bear,
Bless, O God, her from whose womb we came.

Every holiness, blessing and power,
Be yielded to us every time and every hour,
In name of the Holy Threefold above,
Father, Son, and Spirit everlasting.

Be the Cross of Christ to shield us downward,
Be the Cross of Christ to shield us upward,
Be the Cross of Christ to shield us roundward,
Accepting our Beltane blessing from us,
    Accepting our Beltane blessing from us.

Carmina Gadelica 1, p. 189

BLESSING OF THE KINDLING

I will kindle my fire this morning ...

God, kindle Thou in my heart within
A flame of love to my neighbour,
To my foe, to my friend, to my kindred all,
To the brave, to the knave, to the thrall,
O Son of the loveliest Mary,
From the lowliest thing that liveth,
To the Name that is highest of all.

Carmina Gadelica I, p. 231

SMOORING THE FIRE

The sacred Three
To save,
To shield,
To surround
The hearth,
The house,
The household,
This eve,
This night,
Oh! this eve,
This night,
And every night,
Each single night.
    Amen.

Carmina Gadelica I, p. 235

THE OCEAN BLESSING

O Thou who pervadest the heights,
Imprint on us Thy gracious blessing,
Carry us over the surface of the sea,
Carry us safely to a haven of peace,
Bless our boatmen and our boat,
Bless our anchors and our oars,
Each stay and halyard and traveller,
Our mainsails to our tall masts
Keep, O King of the elements in their place
That we may return home in peace ...

Carmina Gadelica 1, p. 325

BLESSINGS

The eye of the great God be upon you,
The eye of the God of glory be on you,
The eye of the Son of Mary Virgin be on you,
The eye of the Spirit mild be on you,
    To aid you and to shepherd you;
Oh the kindly eye of the Three be on you,
    To aid you and to shepherd you.

May the everlasting Father Himself take you
    In His own generous clasp,
    In His own generous arm.

May God shield you on every steep,
May Christ keep you in every path,
May Spirit bathe you in every pass.

May God make safe to you each steep,
May God make open to you each pass,
May God make clear to you each road,
    And may He take you in the clasp of His own two hands.

God's peace be to you,
Jesus' peace be to you,
Spirit's peace be to you
    And to your children,
    Oh to you and to your children,
Each day and night
Of your portion in the world.

The guarding of the God of life be on you,
The guarding of loving Christ be on you,
The guarding of Holy Spirit be on you,
    Every night of your lives,
To aid you and enfold you,
    Each day and night of your lives.

Carmina Gadelica III, pp. 201–207

THE POWER OF GOD

May the strength of God pilot us,
May the power of God preserve us,
May the wisdom of God instruct us,
May the hand of God protect us,
May the way of God direct us,
May the shield of God defend us,
May the host of God guard us
against snares of evil
and the temptations of the world.

St Patrick

IRISH BLESSING

May the road rise to meet you.
May the wind be always at your back.
May the sun shine warm upon your face,
May the rains fall softly on your fields,
And until we meet again,
May God hold you in the palm of His hand.

Irish Journey Blessing

BLESSING

May God the Father bless us;
May Christ take care of us;
May the Holy Spirit enlighten us
all the days of our life.
The Lord be our Defender
and Keeper of body and soul,
both now and forever,
to the ages of ages.

Book of Cerne

Acknowledgements

Extracts from *The Beginnings of Welsh Poetry*, Studies by Sir Ifor Williams, edited by Rachel Browich, are reprinted with permission of the University of Wales Press.

The author and publisher would particularly like to thank the trustees of the *Carmina Gadelica* for their permission to reproduce several extracts from volumes I and III; also to Dr Douglas Grant from the Scottish Academic Press for his invaluable help in ensuring that the extracts were sourced and reproduced correctly.

Extracts from *Celtic Christian Spirituality*, Oliver Davies and Fiona Bowie, SPCK, 1995. Used by permission.

Extract from *Columbanus In His Own Words*, Tomàs O Fiaich, © First published by Veritas Publications. Used with permission.

Extracts from *Irish Litanies*, edited by Charles Plummer, (London, 1925), are reproduced with the kind permission of the Henry Bradshaw Society.

Extracts from *The Poem Book of the Gael*, selected and edited by

Eleanor Hull, Chatto & Windus, reproduced by permission of the Estate of Eleanor Hull and the publisher.

Extracts from *Poems of the Western Highlanders*, G. R. D. McLean, SPCK, 1961. Used by permission. Text copyright of the Estate of the late G. R. D. McLean 1988.

The 'Prayer of St Meryadoc', *Bewnans Meryasek*, quoted in *The Saints of Cornwall*, C. R. John, reproduced by permission of Tor Mark Press, Cornwall.

Poems from *Saltair*, edited by Pádraig Ó Fiannachta, with English translations by Desmond Forristal, are reproduced by permission of The Columba Press, Dublin.

Extract from *Sancti Columbani Opera*, G. S. M. Walker, reproduced by permission of the Governing Board of the School of Celtic Studies of the Dublin Institute for Advanced Studies.

Extracts from *Selections from Ancient Irish Poetry*, translated by Kuno Meyer, are reproduced with permission by Constable Publishers.

Every effort has been made to obtain permission for the copyright material in this anthology. Any amendments will be made in future reprints.

Bibliography

The *Black Book of Carmarthen* dates from around AD 1250, and is thought to have been produced by the monks of St John's Priory, Carmarthen. It includes prayers that date from a much earlier period.

The *Book of Cerne* gets its name from the Benedictine Abbey of Cerne in Dorset: Cerne Abbas. It is a book of personal devotions containing gospel readings with illustrations of the Evangelists, hymns, prayers and other material for personal devotion. It was written in the ninth century (820–40) and most certainly originated in Mercia. The manuscript is now held in the Cambridge University Library.

Browich, Rachel, ed., *The Beginnings of Welsh Poetry*, studies by Sir Ifor Williams, University of Wales Press, 1980.

Carmichael, Alexander, *Carmina Gadelica* (vol. 1, 1900; vol. III, 1940), Scottish Academic Press, Edinburgh.

Cooper, James, *The Reliques of Ancient Scottish Devotions*, Peter Davies Ltd, 1934. (This contains the extract on page 52, which is originally

from *The Book of Deer*. This is a ninth-century book of the four gospels, which originally belonged to the Columban Monastery of Deer in Aberdeenshire. Various prayers are written on spare pages of the gospels.)

Davies, Oliver and Bowie, Fiona, *Celtic Christian Spirituality*, SPCK, 1995.

Hull, Eleanor, (ed.), *The Poem Book of the Gael*, Chatto & Windus, 1913.

John, Catherine R., *The Saints of Cornwall*, Dyllansow Truran, 1981.

Maclean, Alistair, *Hebridean Altars*, Moray Press, 1937.

Mclean, G. R. D., *Poems of the Western Highlanders*, SPCK, 1961.

Meyer, Kuno, tr., *Selections from Ancient Irish Poetry*, Constable Publishers, 1928.

O Fiaich, *Columbanus In His Own Words*, Veritas Publications, 1974.

Ó Fiannachta, Pádraig (ed.), with English translations by Forristal, Desmond, *Saltair*, The Columba Press, 1988.

Plummer, Charles, *Irish Litanies*, Henry Bradshaw Society, 1992.

Van de Weyer, Robert, *Celtic Fire*, Darton, Longman & Todd, 1995.

Walker, G. S. M. (ed.), *Sancti Columbani Opera*, The Dublin Insitute of Advanced Studies, 1970.